Creating
with
Precious
Metal
Clay

By
Jeanette Landenwitch

National Library of Canada Cataloguing in Publication

Landenwitch, Jeanette, 1956-
    Creating with precious metal clay / Jeanette Landenwitch.

Includes index.
ISBN 1-55369-470-8

    1. Precious metal clay. I. Title.

TT213.L36 2002   739.2   C2002-901874-9

TRAFFORD

This book was published *on-demand* **in cooperation with Trafford Publishing.**
On-demand publishing is a unique process and service of making a book available for retail sale to the public taking advantage of on-demand manufacturing and Internet marketing.
On-demand publishing includes promotions, retail sales, manufacturing, order fulfilment, accounting and collecting royalties on behalf of the author.

Suite 6E, 2333 Government St., Victoria, B.C. V8T 4P4, CANADA
Phone   250-383-6864   Toll-free   1-888-232-4444 (Canada & US)
Fax   250-383-6804   E-mail   sales@trafford.com
Web site   www.trafford.com   TRAFFORD PUBLISHING IS A DIVISION OF TRAFFORD HOLDINGS LTD.
Trafford Catalogue #02-0283   www.trafford.com/robots/02-0283.html

10   9   8   7   6   5   4   3   2

I especially thank
my family
for their love and support,
and my wonderful husband,
David,
for his encouragement and patience.

Artist's Statement

I began working with Precious Metal Clay in early 1999 and immediately became intrigued. Since then I have worked extensively with the material, and have completed the program, through the PMC Guild, to achieve my certification for teaching.

I have written this book for my students, and for those who seek to discover the true expression this material allows. Immerse yourself into the spontaneous creativity of the world of PMC. Relax, enjoy, and have fun!

Jeanette Landenwitch
Precious Metal Clay Artist
Certified Instructor

Table of Contents

Forward..8
Introduction...9
Properties of Standard PMC, PMC+, and PMC3...10
Tools and Supplies..13
Using PMC...20
Firing PMC..30
After Firing..34
Designing PMC Pieces...37

Projects

Coil Earrings..40
Textured, Layered Pendant...44
Acorn Mold..50
Beads, Hollow Forms, and Cores..52
      Bead with Paper Towel Core...55
      Dragonfly Vase...58
Carving and Cutwork...62
Simple Bypass Ring..65
Ring Set with Cubic Zirconia..66
Setting Real Stones—Amber...70
Pendant with Highly Dimensional Glass..74
Link Bracelet with Enamel..76
Cuff Bracelet...80
Firing Silver and 24K Gold PMC Together...84
Adding Fired Gold PMC to PMC+...86
PMC Sheet—Pin with Dichroic Glass...90

Special Section for Potters

PMC Applied to Glazed Ceramic Tiles
      High Fire Glaze..94
PMC Applied to Glazed Ceramic Tiles
      Low Fire Glaze..96
PMC 3 Applied to Glazed Ceramic Tiles..98

Resources..100
Index...101

Forward

In the early 1990's Mitsubishi Corporation in Japan developed a product they call Precious Metal Clay (PMC). It was introduced in the United States in 1995. PMC is made up of tiny micron sized particles of silver or gold, suspended in an organic binder. This achieves the clay consistency. When fired in a kiln, the binder burns away, and the metal particles bond and fuse together. The result is an item that is pure precious metal. PMC pieces can be hallmarked as either fine silver-- .999 or F/S—or 24K gold. It is non-toxic and is purchased in clay, paste, paper sheet, or syringe form, ready to use. No measuring or mixing is necessary.

My purpose in writing this book is to teach about the properties and handling of PMC. The tools, methods and techniques I discuss are meant as starting points on which to build. This is a new medium so, in a sense, everyone is a beginner. The techniques I discuss range from the beginner to the advanced levels. The projects I have designed are relatively easy so the artist can concentrate on practicing the techniques. There are empty pages periodically for note taking. As you become more comfortable with PMC you will begin to combine these techniques to make more advanced designs. You'll reach a point where your creativity can't help but take over!

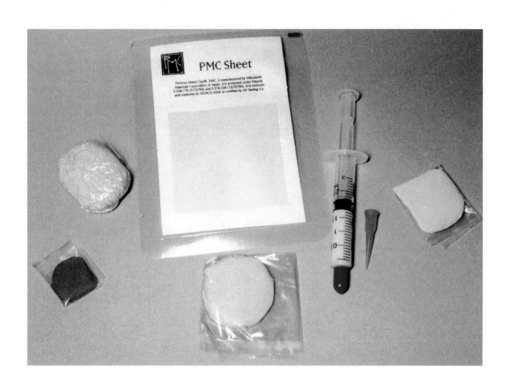

**Forms of PMC, PMC+ and
PMC3 (PMC paste not shown)**

Introduction

PMC is a revolutionary development in the precious metal industry. It allows for easy creation of detail in designs that would be very difficult and painstaking to achieve using conventional forms of metal and methods of working. Expensive tools and equipment are not needed to work with PMC.

It is a very versatile product. The silver and gold PMC can be used separately, or in combination with each other, as in two-tone pieces. PMC can be combined, before firing, with other materials such as potter's clay, sterling silver, high-fired ceramics, synthetic corundum stones, and, after firing, using epoxy, or soldering methods. It can be enameled, carved, or even wheel-thrown. Three dimensional pieces and hollow forms such as beads and vases can easily be made.

PMC is a very 'forgiving' medium. Changes in the piece can be made at any stage of creation, allowing for the design to truly evolve. New designs can be tested with very little time commitment. You will also learn that, with a little vigilance, there is virtually no wasted PMC. Slightly or completely dried PMC can be re-hydrated to working consistency, or made into slip (a paste form of PMC used for joining and repairing).

PMC has incredible potential and limitless possibilities. Your designs can be as simple or as intricate as you desire. As you learn about PMC, your imagination will be more than sparked. You will find yourself thinking of more design ideas than you have time to create. By all means try new things and experiment with new ideas. This is a product that is in its infancy. It has tremendous potential and is very easily individualized. Experienced artisans, jewelers, clay workers, bead-makers, etc., will find ways to incorporate PMC into existing methods of working. Novice hobbyists and budding artisans will have wonderful success from the very beginning. You will find great satisfaction and encouragement when you see the professional results you can achieve. Those who experience PMC will add a dimension to their work that has been unavailable until now.

Properties of Standard PMC, PMC+, and PMC 3

Precious Metal Clay is available in pure silver, and in 24 Karat gold.

There are three types of silver PMC—standard PMC, PMC+ (called PMC Plus), and PMC 3. Each can be worked the same, using the same tools, yet each type also has its own properties and characteristics. These varying qualities are what make using PMC so very versatile. Although each type of silver PMC has its own rate of shrinkage, the shrinkage is uniform throughout the piece. Therefore, the proportion and scale within the piece before it is fired, will remain the same after firing, the piece will just be smaller. Also note that the shrinkage will occur in all directions—length, width, and thickness. One of the beauties of the shrinkage characteristic is that you create the piece in a larger size (definitely a plus for those of us who wear glasses), and the detail becomes more enhanced after it has been fired.

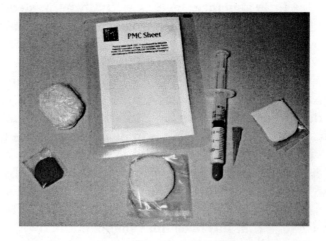

Top to bottom- first column: silver standard PMC, 24K gold PMC
second column: silver PMC+ sheet, PMC+ lump, PMC+ syringe
third column: silver PMC 3

Standard PMC

In standard PMC, whether silver or gold, the binder is about 30% of the content of the silver clay mixture. Since the binder burns away, the piece will be about 70% of the original size after firing. There is a PMC ruler made specifically to help measure the shrinkage of standard PMC. I have found it to be very accurate. (Fig. 1) THIS RULER WORKS FOR STANDARD PMC ONLY, BOTH SILVER AND GOLD. Each side has a true 6" ruler. On one side there is also an expanded ruler that shows the size the piece should be made before firing in order to achieve the intended finished size. For example, if you want a piece to be 1" long when it is finished, then you would use the expanded ruler and actually make the piece the expanded 1". On the reverse side

there is a shrunken ruler. If you are using a mold, for instance, that the size has already been determined, then you would measure that mold with the true 6" ruler and check the shrunken ruler to see what the actual after firing size would be. So, a piece made from a 1" mold before firing would actually end up being ¾" after it is fired.

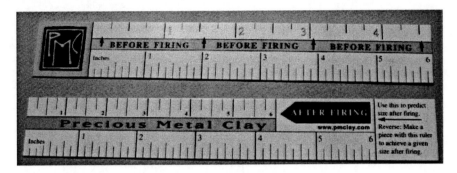

Fig. 1

Standard silver PMC is fired at 1650F for two hours. Gold is fired at 1830F for two hours. After firing, PMC is stronger than the same item made in conventional metal of the same purity. PMC is more porous, therefore resulting in pieces that are lighter in weight than their counterparts in conventional fine silver and 24K gold. This characteristic is particularly advantageous when making larger wearable art items.

PMC+

Silver PMC+ has approximately 12% binder in the content of the clay, and therefore shrinks to about 88% of its original size. It is denser after firing than standard PMC, therefore is slightly heavier. There are three firing temperature and time options for PMC+. It only needs to be fired for 10 minutes, but can be fired longer. When fired for two hours, at 1650F, it becomes almost as strong as sterling silver. (See chapter about Firing). Firing at the lower temperature of 1470F makes it possible to embed sterling silver findings, such as earring posts, before firing.

PMC 3

Silver PMC 3 has the same shrinkage rate as PMC+. PMC 3 can also be fired for as little as 10 minutes, or as long as two hours. If fired for two hours it will become slightly denser than the other two forms of PMC, and, therefore, slightly stronger. If fired for two hours, PMC 3 must first be heated to about 250C for at least 10 minutes to be sure the binder burns away.

Figs. 2 and 3 compare the shrinkage of the three types of PMC.

 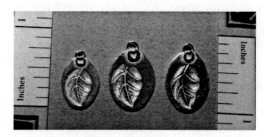

Fig. 2   **Fig. 3**

From left to right: Standard PMC, PMC+, PMC3

No matter which form of PMC you use, after firing it is pure precious metal and can be handled as such. It can be sanded, soldered, polished, tumbled, burnished, oxidized, wire brushed for a satin finish, enameled, etc.

Tools and Supplies

The tools used for PMC are simple and inexpensive. Some of these items you may already have around your house. Plastic and metal tools seem to work best. PMC can be easily removed from them as you work, as well as after it has dried on the tool. Items that are wood, paper, or cardboard have a tendency to absorb the moisture out of the PMC as you are working, therefore, drying it out faster. It is difficult to completely clean dried PMC off of wooden and paper tools.

Some of the most basic tools you will need are shown below– plastic rolling pin, plastic spatula, PMC ruler, dusting brush, slip brush, pick or needle tool (Fig. 4), color shapers, playing cards, plastic sheet. (Fig. 5)

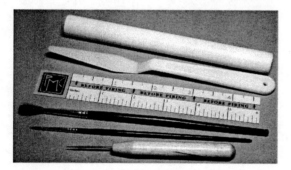

Fig. 4

Fig. 5

You'll need a container of water handy such as a small paper cup. The water is used sparingly to keep the PMC hydrated. Olive oil is also used sparingly on the hands and tools, if necessary, to keep the PMC from sticking. A small airtight container such as a plastic film cylinder or plastic kitchen storage dish is used to keep slip.

Other supplies

PLAYING CARDS are used to establish uniform thickness when rolling out PMC. They are also pliable enough to cut shapes such as arcs, circles, and teardrops from PMC sheet. Other items that can be used to determine uniform thickness are pieces of thin wood, cardboard, or a plastic milk carton cut into strips. (Fig. 6) Cardboard can be used for this purpose because it will not come in contact with the PMC.

Fig. 6

There are many cutting tools available that will easily cut PMC. (Fig. 7) They are be used when the PMC is fresh. Tools such as the regular scissors and decorative scissors can also cut dry PMC.

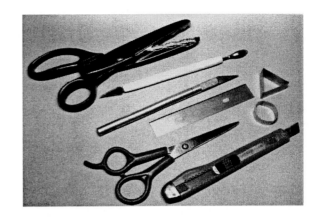

Fig. 7

The sky's the limit when it comes to texturing tools! Some ideas are: a comb, toothbrush, leaves, buttons, lace, paper doilies, screening, screws, nail file, tree bark, rubber stamps, clay cutters. Items such as erasers, craft sticks, toothpicks, and chopsticks can be carved to use as stamping tools. Dowel rods can be carved, or have shapes applied to them, to roll designs into the PMC. Fig. 8 shows some texturing tools.

Fig. 8

Drape PMC over cabochons or plastic artist palettes to shape your piece and achieve a dome shape. The PMC pieces are removed from these tools before firing. (Fig. 9)

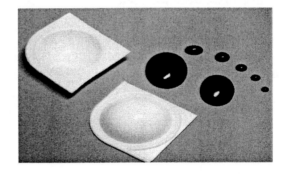

Fig. 9

Sanding sponges, grits fine to microfine, or sandpaper, grits 1000 to 2500, are used to sand rough spots before the piece is fired. Needle files are handy for smaller areas, and to sand the inside of bails. (Fig. 10)

Fig. 10

A plastic needlepoint canvas works well as a drying grid. The grid allows air to circulate around the bottom of the piece as well as the top. (Fig. 11)

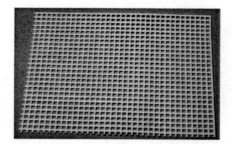

Fig. 11

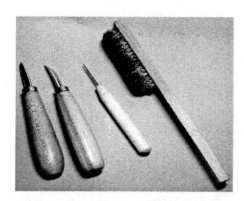

Fig. 12

Fig. 13

There are several ways to finish PMC pieces. Burnishers are used to apply a high polish finish. These hand burnishers, straight and curved, are most effectively used to polish parts of the piece that are to be accented, such as the edges. If the whole piece is to be high polished it is much easier to tumble it in a tumbler with mixed shot and a burnishing liquid. The wire brush is used for a brushed, or satin finish. Either a brass or steel wire brush can be used. The brass brush sometimes leaves a yellow cast on the silver pieces, which can usually be removed with a rouge cloth. (Fig. 12) Fine steel wool (0000) can be used to achieve a brushed finish. Polishing paper, grits 600 to 8000, are used to hand polish to a high shine. Polishing pads give a final polish to the shine. (Fig. 13)

The flat-nose, round-nose and chain-nose jewelry pliers are handy for working wire to join bracelet links together or add pendant bails. (Fig. 14)

Fig. 14

Other supplies that may come in handy are paper, scissors, scotch tape, which can be used for making patterns.

Firing Supplies

The kiln is essential, obviously because PMC must be fired to become pure metal. There are three things to consider when choosing a kiln. It must be able to heat to temperature, it has to hold the temperature constant through the firing time, and it must heat evenly throughout the chamber. There is an electronic kiln that is made for PMC. A jeweler's burnout kiln will also work (more details in Firing section).

Fig. 15

Flat bisque tiles, flower pots and flower pot saucers are used to lay PMC pieces on to place them in the kiln. None of these should have any kind of glaze or finish on them. (Fig. 15) You will need a supply of these because the high temperature of the kiln and the subsequent cooling will cause them to crack after a few uses. I save the cracked pieces and use them to fire smaller sized PMC pieces.

Other supplies you will need are: a very durable, heat proof oven mitt or gloves, long-handled tongs with heat protected handles, a heat-proof surface, such as a brick (or two) to set hot pieces when removed from the kiln, and a small, metal bowl with water, to quench pieces after firing.

Alumina hydrate, a by-product of aluminum, is a fine white powder used to support shaped PMC pieces during firing (available at pottery supply houses). WEAR A MASK AND EYE PROTECTION WHEN USING THIS PRODUCT. DO NOT BREATHE THE DUST. WASH YOUR HANDS THOROUGHLY AFTER USING IT. KEEP IN A TIGHTLY CLOSED GLASS CONTAINER, CLEARLY MARKED AS 'POISONOUS—FOR PMC USE ONLY'. Vermiculite is a more coarsely textured material used to support less delicately shaped and textured PMC pieces. It can be purchased from any gardening store. (Fig. 16)

Fig. 16

Jeweler's investment is a type of plaster that jewelers use. Use the dried plaster without adding liquid, or crush used investment to a powder and use as support material for firing.

OPTIONAL TOOLS AND MATERIALS

Fig. 17 shows some other tools that will add to the fun of working with PMC. They include miniature wood carving tools, 1.5mm, 2mm, 3mm sizes, jeweler's wax carving tools, and extruders such as clay guns with changeable discs, or syringes (some with different sized tips).

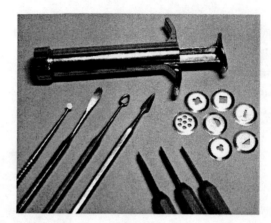

Fig. 17

Using PMC

Work Space

PMC is non-toxic and is very clean and easy to use. You can work with it virtually anywhere. All that is needed is a sturdy, smooth tabletop, good lighting, and preferably no draft from windows, air conditioning units, heaters or fans.

Become Familiar With PMC

When you purchase an ounce of PMC you will get a <u>full ounce</u> of silver. There are 30 grams of silver in an ounce. In a new package of PMC, the ounce will actually weigh about 41.1 grams. The extra weight is the binder. PMC+ comes in a 28 gram jar, has only about 12% binder and a new package weighs 31.6 grams. PMC 3 comes in a 16 gram package, has about 12% binder, and weighs 18 grams new.

Familiarize yourself with the feel of PMC as it comes when you open a fresh package. This is PMC in its best workable consistency. It is malleable to the touch without being sticky, or cracking. In best working conditions (meaning no air blowing around) PMC has a working time of about 15-20 minutes before it will begin to dry out. Therefore, you will need to keep it hydrated as you work. To do this, periodically dab your fingertip into water and rub a drop or two over the clay, particularly the edges. Because the water is gradually absorbed by the PMC only a very little bit is needed. Using too much water will make the PMC sticky. The excess should be dabbed off. If puddles are left to sit on the PMC, they will gradually be absorbed and you will notice your design begin to "mush out". As it dries large cracks will be more likely to develop because the piece will not be drying uniformly enough.

A thin layer of olive oil applied to hands and tools helps to keep the PMC from sticking. The residual oil that rubs off onto the PMC can also help to seal the clay so it doesn't dry out as quickly as it is worked. After the PMC has been rolled out, laying a piece of saran wrap over the portion that is not immediately in use helps to keep it from drying too quickly.

As I mentioned earlier, there is virtually no waste with PMC. Design changes can be made at any stage in the design process. PMC that has partially or completely dried out can be *re-hydrated* to its original consistency, or made into *slip,* and used again.

Re-hydrating PMC

First, cut the dried PMC into small pieces. The smaller the pieces the faster the PMC will absorb the water. (Fig. 18)

Fig. 18

Add enough water to get the PMC wet. Let it sit for 10 to 15 minutes. The PMC will begin to soften as the water is absorbed. (Fig. 19)

Fig. 19

Fig. 20

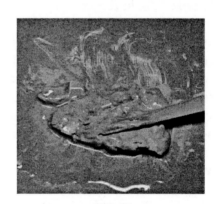

Fig. 21

With the plastic spatula, work the water into the clay as much as possible, working out any lumps. Wrap the PMC in plastic wrap. Check the PMC after a couple of hours. It takes time for the water to be fully absorbed. If the PMC is sticky and mushy, let it dry out some. If it is a little dry, dab some water on it, and, holding the PMC in the plastic wrap, work the water into it. Check to make sure all the lumps are gone. Continue this process until the clay is back to its workable consistency. (Figs. 20, 21)

Making Slip

Slip is PMC with a little bit more water added to make a paste. (Fig. 22) It can be used to make joins, to embellish, to fill in cracks that have occurred while drying, or to repair PMC pieces. PMC can be purchased in slip, or paste, form, or you can make your own. To start your own slip jar, take a small amount of PMC, put it in a small, plastic container. Add a drop or two of water at a time, mixing it until it is a toothpaste consistency. As you work you will find small pieces of PMC laying around your work space that have dried out. Put these into your slip container. Add a few drops of water, as needed, to your slip to keep a good consistency. When sanding PMC there will be PMC dust that will accumulate on the table. This dust should also be added to the slip jar. With a little bit of care and vigilance, there is virtually no waste with PMC.

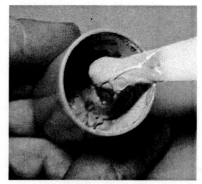

Fig. 22

Forming Techniques

To make a *sheet* of PMC, pinch the amount of clay you will need from the one ounce package. Immediately rewrap the unused portion in the plastic to prevent unnecessary drying. Place the PMC onto a clear plastic sheet. Determine the thickness needed, then place the necessary number of cards (or whatever tool is being used to determine an even thickness) on either side of the PMC. Place the ends of the plastic rolling pin on the card stack and roll out the PMC into a sheet. (Fig. 23) Also keep your hands at the ends of the rolling pin. This will keep the heaviest pressure off of the PMC, will allow you to roll a more even thickness, and the PMC will be less likely to stick to the plastic sheet.

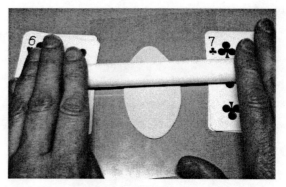

Fig. 23

To make a round *wire,* roll a piece of PMC out evenly, as if making a long 'snake'. (Fig. 24) Make it any thickness you need. PMC can also be extruded from a syringe, using varying sized tips to acquire different sized wires.

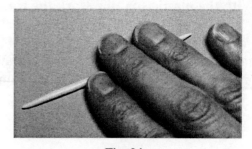

Fig. 24

Fig. 25   Fig. 26   Fig. 27

To make square wires, cut thin, square strips from a PMC sheet. (Figs. 25, 26, 27)

Joining

There are basically three ways in which PMC parts and pieces can be joined before firing. They are: fresh PMC to fresh PMC, fresh PMC to dried PMC, and dried PMC to dried PMC. Here are the methods for each:

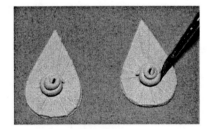

Fig. 28

1) **Fresh PMC to fresh PMC (Fig. 28)** -- The method of joining fresh PMC is the easiest. Lay one piece on top of another and apply gentle pressure, if necessary. This may be all that is needed for the parts to remain joined after firing, but it can't be guaranteed. To absolutely ensure a successful join, use a small paintbrush and apply a small amount of water where the two parts meet each other. You will be able to see the PMC "melt" together, very slightly, where it has been joined. Remove excess water using either the paintbrush to soak it up, or paper towel or tissue.

Remember not to 'puddle' the water on your piece. If standing water is left on the piece it could very well develop large cracks that will have to be filled in later. If done correctly, the PMC will feel firmly attached when touched.

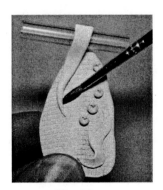

Fig. 29

2) **Fresh PMC to dried PMC (Fig. 29)** – There are two ways to ensure strong joins when joining fresh PMC with dried PMC. The first is the same technique as described for joining fresh to fresh. The difference being that initially you may have to use a little more water so that the fresh PMC sufficiently "melts" onto the dried PMC. It is a very slight, but important, "melting" that occurs. You will know it is a good join because you will see a very good adherence of the fresh PMC onto the dried PMC, and it will feel solid. This method works especially well when joining smaller, more intricate parts. Again, remember to remove excess water.

The second method of joining fresh with dried PMC utilizes PMC slip. Use this method when joining larger parts together. (Fig. 30) First, rough up the area on the dried PMC where the join will occur. This will help to facilitate a mechanical join which will guarantee a successful, strong connection. Next, add a touch of water, and then slip, to the same roughed up area. Add the fresh PMC part. Apply gentle pressure to unite the parts. Wipe off any excess slip that seeps out.

Fig. 30

3) Dried PMC to dried PMC -- Joins can be made after each of the PMC parts has dried. Add a drop of water to the area where the join will occur. Apply PMC slip to one of the areas. (Fig. 31) Press the parts together. (Fig. 32) Make sure the join is solid and clean all the way around. Wipe away any slip that has seeped out. It is easiest to clean the join now rather than try to sand it after it has dried.

Fig. 31

Fig. 32

Joins can also be made after two parts have been fired. Hold the two pieces together and apply fresh PMC. Since the PMC will shrink during firing, the process may have to be repeated in order to get a good, solid adhesion. After you're satisfied that the join is secure, refine it by filing it smooth with a metalsmith file. Consider using PMC+ for this method since it shrinks less and is stronger than standard PMC. This technique can also be used to repair PMC pieces.

Texturing, Embellishing, Folding, Draping

Texturing, embellishing, folding, and draping are the essence of PMC. It is so much fun, incredibly fascinating and has limitless possibilities. Texturing can be done after the piece has dried, by carving or scratching. PMC can be pressed from molds, or textured with decorative rollers. It can be extruded from a syringe or clay gun directly onto your piece. Virtually any item can be used to press designs into the fresh PMC. Items that are more fragile, intricate, and combustible, can be pressed into the PMC and left in during the firing. They will burn away leaving their exact impressions. This method will create one-of-a-kind designs (for the obvious reason that the texturing item will burn up during firing). Fig. 33 shows a combination of several of these techniques.

Fig. 33

There are different sized tips available for the syringe so it's possible to extrude even very fine lines. A variety of discs come with clay guns. These shapes can be extruded, then cut into small thickness and applied to your piece. Or cut your own shapes and designs and apply them. To add further interest, besides texturing and embellishing, PMC can be stretched, compressed, or rolled up, adding further dimension to your work.

Three Dimensional and Hollow Pieces

Cores and core materials

When a three dimensional, hollow piece is made a core needs to be created. The core will act as a support for the piece as you work, as the piece dries, and in some cases when the piece is fired. There are non-removable cores and removable cores.

Removable cores will be taken out of the piece before firing (Fig. 34). ONLY IF YOU ARE SURE YOU WILL REMOVE THE CORE BEFORE FIRING CAN YOU USE AN ITEM THAT WILL NOT BURN UP.

Fig. 34

Non-removable cores will remain inside the piece and will burn up during firing (Fig. 35). Whenever possible cores that are non-toxic should be used for this purpose. Some ideas for core materials are: bread, noodles, crackers, cereal, tissues or paper towels. Styrofoam can be purchased in existing sizes and shapes, or you can cut and shape your own cores from a slab. However, it will give off toxic fumes when fired, so the kiln will need to be well vented or set outside.

Fig. 35

Paper clay makes a great core for larger beads or flat hollow pieces, but doesn't shrink during firing. Therefore, a layer about 1/8" thick needs to be added around the paper clay to allow for the shrinkage of the PMC. Several layers of wet paper towels or tissues can be wrapped around the paper clay core, then let dry. However, some shapes do not warrant this technique. Therefore, as I learned from my Certification Instructor, the paper clay cores can also be built up with layers of wax. (Fig. 36)

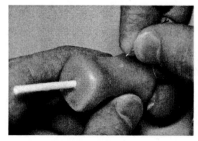

Fig. 36

I've had limited success with paper mache- like products, however, there are a couple of unique characteristics that I thought would be worth mentioning. There is a commercially made form of paper mache that comes in a dry, block form, and can be purchased at your local craft store. Simply add water until it has a consistency that does not stick to your hands. Mold it to any shape and size. Allow for slight shrinkage as it dries. It dries rock hard and can be sanded. It does hold its shape during firing, so provides support throughout the firing process, yet after firing it crumbles like ashes and can be easily removed from the piece.

Fig. 37

IT IS IMPORTANT TO NOTE THAT GREAT CARE MUST BE TAKEN WHEN THIS TYPE OF PAPER MACHE IS USED AS A NON-REMOVABLE CORE. FIRING SUCCESS CANNOT BE GUARANTEED. ALL OF THESE PIECES WERE MADE FROM STANDARD PMC, AND FIRED AT 1650F FOR TWO HOURS. (FIGS.37, 38, 39)

If used as a non-removable core in a closed piece, then no more than three small pieces (1" or less) should be fired at the same time. Otherwise too much heat will be generated as this type of core burns, and your PMC pieces will melt and deform (Fig. 37). It's like creating a miniature bon fire that raises the temperature inside the kiln. The same situation would occur if your PMC piece was an open design, such as a vase, had this material as a non-removable core, and was placed in firing support material (alumina hydrate or vermiculite). With the firing support material on the outside of your piece and the paper mache core on the inside, the heat is trapped, builds up, and will melt the part of the piece that is sandwiched between the two (Fig. 38). I've also not had luck with pieces 2" or larger, even if the piece is not enclosed in the back. (Fig. 39) Even at lower firing temperatures success cannot be guaranteed. I would suggest the best use for this type of material is as a removable core.

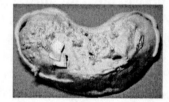
Fig. 38

Fig. 39

Refining PMC Pieces

After you have completely constructed the piece, it will be fired. The PMC doesn't necessarily *have* to dry before firing, but there are definitely advantages in doing so. Keep in mind that:

1) Cracks that develop while drying can be filled in and sanded before firing. It is much easier to do this before firing than after.

2) The edges can be refined and sanded smooth.

3) If a thick piece is not completely dry, it could end up developing an unplanned bulge because the binder will not be able to escape quickly enough during the firing process.

After your PMC piece has dried it is in its *'leather hard'* or *'green stage'*. Check all edges for roughness. Any rough edges should be sanded smooth because after PMC is fired it is all metal and edges that are not rounded off will be sharp. This is particularly important for jewelry, so it is comfortable to wear and won't snag clothing. While it is possible to break the PMC if *too* much pressure is applied, PMC in this stage is surprisingly durable. Flat PMC sheets may even have some flexibility to them. You will find the pieces easy to hold and work with while sanding and refining.

To refine PMC pieces use sandpaper or sanding sponges. Sand all rough edges. 1000 grit sandpaper, or the fine grit sanding sponge is a good place to start. Progress through to the finer grits as needed. It doesn't take much pressure or sanding to achieve a smooth, finished edge. (Fig. 40) The piece is now ready to be fired. (Brush the silver PMC dust into the slip jar). Note: Even though it is easier to refine the PMC before it is fired, it doesn't necessarily *have* to be. Since PMC is pure precious metal after it is fired, it can be filed and refined with the same metalsmith techniques as used for conventional metal.

Fig. 40

If a PMC piece won't be fired immediately, it can be stored off to the side where it won't be damaged. There is no time frame in which PMC *has* to be fired.

Repairing with PMC

If cracks developed in the PMC as it dried, it is easy to repair them before the piece is fired. (Fig. 41) Simply fill them with either slip or with fresh PMC, let it dry, then sand until the surface is smooth and blends nicely with the design. (Fig. 42) Fire as usual.

Fig. 41

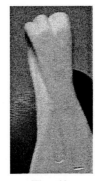

Fig. 42

To repair PMC pieces that have already been fired use the same technique as pre-fired PMC. Fill the cracks in with PMC or PMC+, let it dry, smooth it off, then re-fire. The difference is that during the re-firing, the PMC or PMC+ will shrink. Therefore, you may have to do more than one application and re-firing in order to fully repair the cracks. PMC+ or PMC 3 might lend themselves a little more favorably to repair jobs than standard PMC, because they shrink less during firing, and are stronger after firing.

Soldering PMC

With a little practice PMC can be successfully soldered. Since PMC is more porous than conventional precious metal, the solder will tend to 'soak in' rather quickly. It will help to first burnish the spot where the solder will be applied. As soon as the piece is heated to the temperature where the solder flows, immediately remove the flame. PMC can be pickled. Again, because of its porosity, it should be thoroughly cleaned afterward either in an ultrasonic machine, or by soaking in a solution of baking soda and water in order to neutralize the pickling acid.

Care of PMC

PMC is easy to care for. It does not tarnish or get dirty as readily as other metals. Simply clean the pieces with a silver or gold polishing cloth. Jewelry cleaners can be used, with care, depending upon the finish on the piece, and any stones that may have been set into the piece. After cleaning, rinse the piece thoroughly to expel any remaining chemicals.

Firing PMC

The firing process is easy to master. The three critical elements needed to ensure a successful firing are temperature, time, and even heat.

1) the kiln must be able to hold a consistent firing temperature,
2) it must be capable of holding the temperature for up to two hours, and
3) it *must* fire uniformly. Even though, technically, the size of the kiln is not critical, a smaller kiln will have a smaller chamber and will be more efficient to use. What is most important is that there are no cold or hot spots within the chamber.

Important Firing Considerations

Full temperature needs to be reached in order for the sintering process to properly occur. By the time the full firing temperature is reached, the binder in the clay will have burned away. What will remain are the silver or gold metal particles. While the kiln is at full temperature the sintering process for the metal will occur. This means that the particles will reach a liquified state (not as high as melting point), in which they will fuse and bond together. If the kiln temperature goes higher than the required firing temperature, then the melting temperature of the metal could be reached. As a result your PMC creation will become deformed, come out looking like melted, crumpled tin foil , or melt into a blob. On the other hand, if the temperature is not high enough, the sintering process cannot sufficiently occur, and the metal particles will not be able to adequately bond. This will result in a weak, easily breakable piece.

It is also critical to fire PMC for the *minimum specified time*. If the pieces are not fired long enough, the sintering process will not be complete. Again, the pieces will be weak and easily broken. If the pieces are fired longer than the specified time, it will not hurt them. PMC can also be fired more than once without causing harm as long as the specified firing temperature is not exceeded. This lends PMC to be successfully used with other medium such as enamels, fused glass, certain earthen clays, etc.

Finally, the kiln *must* fire uniformly, with no cold or hot spots within the chamber. The cold or hot spots will have the same effect as not having the correct firing temperature throughout the firing process. The PMC pieces could end up being either over fired or under fired.

Kiln Set-up

The kiln should be set up where there will be good ventilation, and air circulation around it. It should not be placed too close to walls or closed in areas. Have a heat-proof surface next to the kiln where you can set the hot pieces as they are being removed for cooling. I have a small platform of two to four bricks right next to my kiln. Have all of the tools you use for the kiln near you and ready to go. The last thing you want to do is leave the hot kiln unattended while you search for something you need. Have a small, metal bowl filled with water readily available in order to *quench* your pieces after firing. You will need enough water to immerse the pieces completely. (To quench pieces simply drop them into water and they cool immediately. CAUTION: Only PMC pieces that do NOT have embedded items should be quenched).

Preparing PMC Pieces for Firing

PMC is non-toxic when fired. It does not need to be vented for fumes, unless other materials, such as a styrofoam core, are used that give off toxic fumes when burned.

Pieces that are not completely dry must be placed in a cold kiln. As long as the PMC pieces aren't very thick, the time that it takes for the kiln to ramp up to temperature is usually adequate to allow for the escape of steam as the remaining binder material evaporates. If these pieces were placed into a hot kiln, the binder would not be able to escape properly, and the result would be unwanted bulges or misshaped pieces. I would highly recommend that layered pieces or very thick pieces be thoroughly dry before attempting to fire them. As a general rule, if the PMC pieces are completely dry before firing, the chances for consistent successful firings will increase.

Completely dried pieces can be placed in a cold or hot kiln. Obviously it is safer to place pieces in a cold kiln because of the intense heat of the firing temperatures.

Flat PMC pieces are simply laid on a flat tile, and the tile is then placed in the kiln. The pieces can be very close to each other, but not touching. Because they shrink during firing they will pull away from each other and will, therefore, not stick together. Shaped pieces can be laid on a bed of support material that has been piled on the tile. (Fig. 43)

Fig. 43

To prepare non-flat or shaped pieces for firng, you can also use a bisque flower pot saucer. Support material, either alumina hydrate or vermiculite, will be placed around and/or under the pieces, to support them during firing. If the piece has fine detail or shaping, then use the alumina hydrate. It has a fine powdery consistency that will support intricate detailing. Vermiculite has a coarser texture and is best used for less detailed, larger pieces or hollow forms. Because of the coarse texture of vermiculite, pieces sometimes will 'sag' in between the vermiculite particles and become misshapen.

Wearing a mask and goggles, spoon alumina hydrate or vermiculite onto the saucer or tile. Set the piece on it making sure all critical areas are supported. If the bottom of the piece needs to remain flat, then set the PMC piece onto the saucer and spoon alumina hydrate around the piece where it needs support. It is not recommended to cover piece or place the support materials inside it. Again, if there is more than one piece, they can be placed close to each other, but not touching. (Fig. 44)

Fig. 44

For a taller piece, such as a vase, use an appropriately sized flowerpot (Fig. 42). Put a piece of flat tile in the bottom to cover the hole, place the PMC piece into the flowerpot. Spoon the support material into the flowerpot and around the PMC piece. Since the PMC will shrink, allow room at the top of the support material for the piece to shrink down without becoming distorted. The support material does not alter during firing. This means that as the PMC piece shrinks, the firing support material (alumina hydrate or vermiculite) won't get out of its way. Instead the PMC will conform to the shape of the support material. When firing is complete the alumina hydrate and vermiculite can be saved and reused indefinitely.

Fig. 45

Used jeweler's investment that has been crushed into powder can also be used for support material in place of alumina hydrate.

Loading the kiln

Place the prepared pieces into the kiln. If only flat tiles are being used, they can be stacked using appropriately sized spacers. Bisque tiles will crack and break after only a few uses, due to the intense heating and cooling involved in the firing process. For this reason I don't recommend stacking them. Soldering tiles are generally safe to stack. Other types of shelving that will not crack, such as used in potter's kilns, are also safe to stack.

Operating the kiln

Follow the kiln's operating instructions. Using the chart below, set the kiln for the appropriate temperature and firing time. Start the kiln.

	Fahrenheit	Centigrade	Time
Standard Gold PMC	1830	1000	2 Hours
Standard Silver PMC	1650	900	2 Hours
Silver PMC+	1650	900	10 Minutes
	1560	850	20 Minutes
	1470	800	30 Minutes
Silver PMC 3	1290	700	10 Minutes
	1200	650	20 Minutes
	1110	600	30 Minutes

IMPORTANT NOTE: PMC+ and PMC 3 fired at 1650F for two hours will achieve a strength very close to that of sterling silver.

When firing is complete, turn the kiln off (unless it does so automatically). The kiln will begin to cool. PIECES THAT HAVE MATERIALS EMBEDDED IN THEM SHOULD BE ALLOWED TO COOL GRADUALLY IN THE KILN SO THERE IS LESS CHANCE THAT CRACKING OR BREAKING OCCURS. Otherwise the door can be opened slightly so it will cool a little faster. The pieces will be glowing orange because of the intense heat, but this will quickly disappear as they cool. Now you can either let them cool in the kiln, or, using the long-handled tongs and heat proof oven mitt, take the pieces out and *quench* them in water.

The pieces are now ready to be finished.

Special firing considerations

Firing two-tone or multiple part PMC pieces

There are two ways to make a two-tone silver and gold PMC piece. The first method is to embed previously fired gold PMC into fresh silver PMC. Since PMC can be safely fired more than once, the gold PMC can be fired at its normal temperature, then embedded into fresh silver PMC and re-fired at the silver firing temperature. The important thing to remember is that *you will be using the finished sizes of previously fired pieces and adding them to unfired PMC that will shrink.* The previously fired parts must be attached in such a way as to ensure they will stay together after firing. The best way to do this is to create a mechanical join. There should be something created on the part to be added, that the unfired PMC can 'grab onto' as it shrinks during firing. This could be in the form of a small ledge, or small cuts, or possibly a hole or two poked into the part. **IF PREVIOUSLY FIRED SILVER IS EMBEDDED INTO FRESH GOLD PMC IT <u>MUST</u> BE FIRED AT THE SILVER FIRING TEMPERATURE. THE GOLD FIRING TEMPERATURE WILL MELT THE SILVER.** Being fired at the silver firing temperature, the gold will reach 90% of its strength.

The second method is to make the entire piece using both the silver and gold PMC, then fire it. In this case the piece *must* be fired at the silver PMC temperature. This is because the gold firing temperature will exceed the melting point temperature of the silver. Special consideration should be taken in designing this kind of two-tone piece. Being fired at the silver firing temperature, the gold will reach 90% of its strength. To be safe, the physical strength of the design should lie in the silver part being able to support the gold part. In other words, design the piece so that the silver will be used for the "high stress" parts of the design, such as the bail.

When combining standard silver PMC with silver PMC+ or PMC 3, use the firing temperature and time for whichever type of PMC is dominant in the piece. Remember, there is a difference in shrinkage between standard PMC, PMC+, and PMC 3. This should be considered when designing the piece.

PMC pieces that aren't two-tone can also be constructed in stages. If adding silver parts to silver, you would use the appropriate firing times and temperatures for the type of silver PMC being used. If adding gold parts to gold, you would use the gold PMC firing time and temperature for each gold firing.

After Firing

After firing, the PMC pieces are solid precious metal and can be finished the same as conventional metal would be. Straight from the kiln the silver PMC will have a white, powdery look, the gold will have a yellow, powdery look.

There are many finishes that can be applied. The finishes we will use are the satin or brushed finish, the high polish finish, the oxidized finish, and enamel. Another option is to leave the PMC piece with the white powdery look as it comes from the kiln.

High Polish Finish

PMC can be polished in a tumbler. This method polishes the entire piece to a high shine. Put stainless steel mixed shot into the tumbler barrel, along with a burnishing liquid, and the PMC pieces. Run the tumbler for at least an hour to achieve a beautiful high shine. (Fig. 46)

Fig. 46

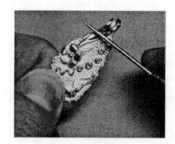

There are two hand methods that can be used if only part of the piece will be accented with a high polish finish. One way is to rub the piece with polishing papers. Start with the 600 grit and progress through to the 8000 grit. The other way is to use a burnisher. Rub the part of the PMC piece to be accented, such as the edges, with the burnisher until it has a high shine. Follow up each of these two methods with a polishing pad, and finally, a polishing cloth. (Fig. 47)

Fig. 47

Professional polishing machines and small rotary tools can also be used, along with various polishing compounds, e.g. tripoli, white diamond, and rouge. Excess polishing compound can be removed by washing with a soft toothbrush and soapy water. Since the PMC is more porous than conventional metal, use the polishing compounds sparingly so as not to cause an embedded buildup.

Satin Finish

To achieve a satin finish, rub the PMC piece with a wire brush, very fine 0000 steel wool, or scotch-brite pads. A steel brush works well for silver. (Fig. 48) A brass brush can be used but may leave a yellow cast, which can be cleaned off with a rouge cloth.

Fig. 48

Oxidizing

A good way to emphasize the detail and texturing in your PMC pieces is to patina, or oxidize, them. (Fig. 49) There are several oxidizing solutions available. I've had great success with liver of sulphur. Whichever solution you choose, follow the instructions included with that solution. First, finish the piece, then patina the piece, and finally, with a fine 1200 grit sandpaper or polishing pad, rub the desired amount of patina off in order to achieve the desired look. Lastly, use a polishing cloth for the final polish.

Fig. 49

Enameling

Fig. 50

Since PMC is Fine Silver it is excellent for enameling. Make and complete your PMC piece as usual. Apply the desired finish. Then enamel the piece.

Applying Findings

Findings such as earring posts, bails, pin backs, etc. can be added after the piece has been fired. They can be applied using a two-part epoxy (follow the instructions on the package). Or, they can be soldered. The soldering process is the same as with conventional metals, with a few considerations. PMC is more porous than conventional metals, so the solder will tend to 'soak in'. PMC+ and PMC 3 are denser than standard PMC and, therefore, easier to solder. Whichever type of PMC is being soldered, burnishing the area where the soldering will occur will close the pores and help reduce the amount that soaks in. PMC can be pickled, but may absorb and hold the pickling acid. To neutralize the acid, clean the piece in an ultrasonic machine, or boil in a weak solution of baking soda and water, for 10-15 minutes.

Fig. 50
Enameled bracelet

Designing PMC Pieces

Inspiration for designing your PMC pieces can be found everywhere. This medium is so versatile that almost any idea you come up with can be successfully transformed into a beautiful work of art. You can make simple, fast, and easily constructed designs, as well as whimsical, formal, informal, and intricate pieces. All the elements of design can be applied: shape, form, texture, contrast, line, positive/negative space.

As you design your pieces keep the order of construction in the back of your mind. Some pieces can be made in one sitting. Others need to be made in stages. Some parts might need to be dry or partially dry before other parts are attached. Some parts need to be made from fresh PMC in get the texturing or shaping effect you want. Some parts might need to be fired before being embedded into fresh PMC, others may be soldered together.

Designs can be tested using polymer clay because it won't dry out. This way you can work out the best design process before starting with the PMC. Make stamping tools and molds with the polymer clay.

Precious Metal Clay allows you to truly work spontaneously.

Good luck, and most of all—*HAVE FUN AND ENJOY!*

Ring set with Cubic Zirconia (pg. 66)

Setting real stones-Amber (pg. 70)

Pendant set with highly dimensional glass (pg. 74)

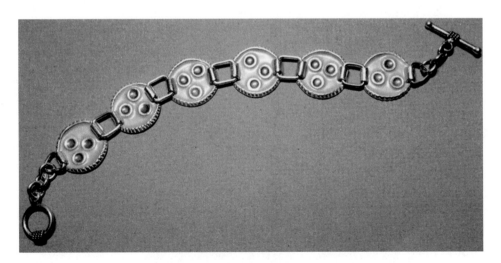

Link bracelet with enamel (pg. 76)

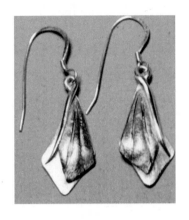

Firing silver and 24K gold PMC together
(pg. 84)

Adding fired gold PMC to PMC+
(pg. 86)

Dichroic glass pin using PMC sheet
(pg. 90)

Projects

Although each project in this section is designed to teach certain techniques, I have also left room for you to express your own style and creativity. Amounts of PMC used will fluctuate depending upon the size you choose to make your piece, and the embellishments added. Now, experience the essence of Precious Metal Clay.

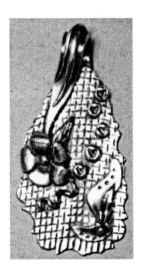

Coil Earrings
Standard Silver PMC

The purpose of this project:

⇒ to become familiar with the feel of PMC
⇒ to form sheets and wires from PMC
⇒ to join fresh PMC to fresh PMC

Rub a thin layer of olive oil onto a plastic sheet. Roll out a sheet of PMC 5 cards thick. As you roll, place the pressure of your hands on the ends of the rolling pin as opposed to the center. This will help to keep the PMC from sticking to the plastic sheet. (Fig. 51)

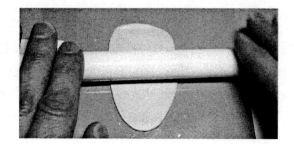

Fig. 51

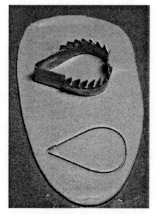

Fig. 52

Using a clay cutter that is about 1" in length, cut two identical pieces from the PMC sheet. Remove the excess PMC by simply lifting it off of the plastic sheet. (Fig. 52)

With any straight tool, impress lines around the cut shapes. These lines should go no more that 1/3 of the depth of the thickness of the PMC. If the impression is too deep will cause a thin spot that could be easily broken after it has been fired. Remember that the PMC will be metal after it is fired, and, like any metal, the thinner it is the more susceptible it will be to bending and breaking. (Fig. 53)

Fig. 53

Roll out a thin wire of PMC. It will be coiled and placed onto the center of the cut pieces so it should be fairly thin, 1/8" to 1/16" thick. (Fig. 54)

Fig. 54

Fig. 55

Roll the PMC wire into a coil. (Fig. 55)

Add a drop of water to the area where the coil will be placed. The water will facilitate a join that will be strong and, if done correctly, the two parts will not come apart after firing. (Fig. 56)

Fig. 56

Lay the coils onto the moistened areas and gently press being careful not to squash them. Then, using a small brush, add some water to the edges of the coil. You should be able to see the two parts very slightly "melt" together, and the coil should be firm and not move when touched. Then you will know that the join will be strong after firing. Be sure to remove any excess water from around the coil. (Figs. 57, 58)

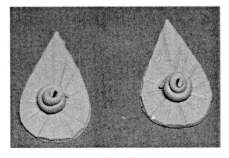

Fig. 57

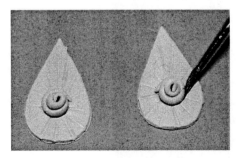

Fig. 58

For this particular shape I've trimmed the point off of the top. It looks more attractive and will let the earrings hang more freely on the earwires. (Fig. 59)

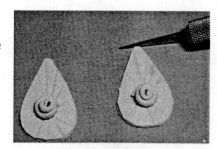

Fig. 59

Roll out two more PMC wires, each about 1/8" thick and 1 ½" long. Shape them so they will form a loop when attached to the main PMC pieces. (Fig. 60) Add a small amount of water to the earring sections in the area where the bails will be added. Add the bails using the same technique as for the coils. Check to make sure the join is strong. Remove excess water.

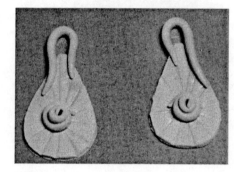

Fig. 60

Set the earrings aside to dry.

Fig. 61

After the earrings are completely dry sand all rough areas smooth. Use a fine grit sanding sponge, or 1000 grit sandpaper. (Fig. 61)

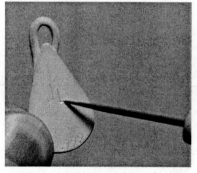

Fig. 62

Using a needle tool, inscribe your initials on the back, and hallmark the earrings .999 or F/S to show that they are Fine Silver. (Fig. 62)

Using the 'before firing' side of the PMC ruler, measure the size of the earrings. The total length of these earrings measures about 1", which is the actual size they will be after firing. (Fig. 63)

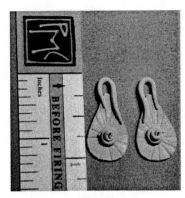

Fig. 63

Place the earrings on a flat tile and fire them at 1650F for two hours. When firing is complete the kiln can be let to cool naturally, or, after the orange glow is gone, the earrings can be taken out and dipped in water to quench them.

Using the 'after firing' side of the PMC ruler measure the earrings. They measure about 1". (Fig. 64)

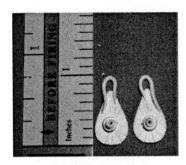

Fig. 64

Straight out of the kiln the earrings have a white powdery look. You can leave this finish if you like. (Fig. 65)

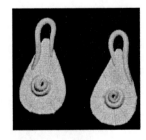

Fig. 65

Tumble them for 1 to 2 hours, oxidize, then add earwires. (Fig. 66)

Fig. 66

Textured, Layered Pendant
Standard Silver PMC

The purpose of this project:

⇒ to experiment with texturing and shaping the PMC.
⇒ to learn how and when to vary the thickness of the PMC
⇒ to learn how to use PMC efficiently

When planning a layered piece there are a few points to keep in mind. Even though PMC is as much as 20% lighter than conventional Fine Silver, the weight of the finished piece should be considered for wearing comfort. With each layer that is added the piece will become thicker and heavier. Therefore, varying thickness should be used. The amount of texturing, shaping, and forming will determine the thickness of each layer. If a layer will have deep texturing a thicker layer is needed. If the PMC part will be shaped and formed, roll out a thinner layer. As a side note, there is also a direct correlation between the thickness of the layers used, and how far the ounce of PMC will go.

To begin this project, rub a thin layer of olive oil onto a plastic sheet. Roll out a sheet of PMC 4 cards thick. This will be the base layer of your pendant. Texture the base layer. (Figs. 67, 68)

Fig. 67

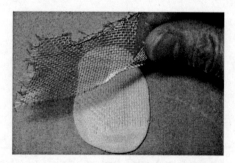

Fig. 68

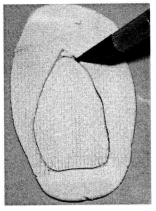

Fig. 69

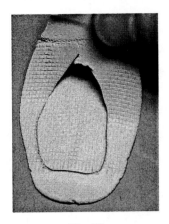

Fig. 70

Cut the desired shape. Remove the excess PMC. (Figs. 69, 70)

Cut a freeform shape and add it to the pendant. Roll several little balls of PMC. Add them to the pendant, and press a small stamp design into them. Remember to use small amounts of water when adding the layers, to be sure they will adhere strongly. Let the pendant dry. After the pendant is completely dry the bail will be added. (Figs. 71, 72)

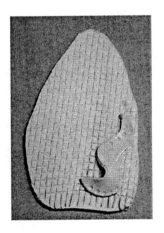

Fig. 71

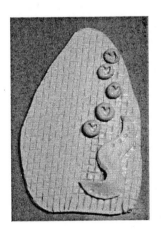

Fig. 72

Adding the Bail

Keeping in mind that during firing the diameter of the bail will shrink along with the rest of the piece, determine the 'before firing' size of the bail for the size of neck chain you will be using with the pendant.

Roll a wire of PMC about 1/8" wide and at least 4" long. (Fig. 73)

Fig. 73

Using a rolling pin, partially flatten the wire. (Fig. 74)

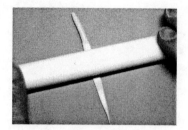

Fig. 74

Lay the bail onto the front of the pendant and over a support that will give you your pre-determined bail size. I used a drinking straw here. The straw will support the bail until it dries. Using a small amount of water, secure the bail to the pendant. (Fig. 75)

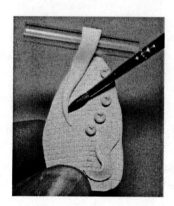

Fig. 75

Carefully turn the pendant over to the back. Dab water onto the spot where the bail will be attached. Attach the bail to the back and trim it off. (Fig. 76)

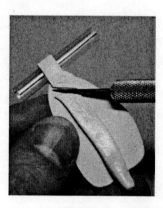

Fig. 76

Stamp a design onto the end of the bail to help secure it to the back. Set the pendant aside to allow the bail to dry. (Fig. 77)

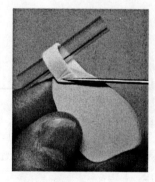

Fig. 77

After the bail has completely dried, use a decorative scissors to trim the edges of the pendant. (Figs. 78, 79)

Fig. 78

Fig. 79

Finish layering the pendant. Let it dry. Using a fine sanding sponge, or 1000 grit sandpaper, sand all rough edges smooth. Remove the drinking straw. Using a needle tool, inscribe your initials, and hallmark .999 or F/S. (Figs. 80, 81)

Fig. 80

Fig. 81

Using the 'Before Firing' PMC ruler I can tell that the pendant will be about 1 3/8" long after it is fired. (Fig. 82)

Fig. 82

Place the pendant on a flat tile and fire it at 1650F for two hours.

After firing finish the pendant with a steel brush. (Fig. 83)

Fig. 83

Burnish the details and edges to a high polish. (Fig. 84)

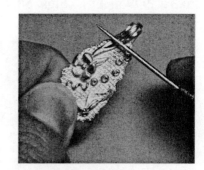

Fig. 84

Acorn Mold

Standard PMC, PMC+, or PMC3

The purpose of this project:

> ⇒ to work with PMC and an existing mold
> ⇒ to learn to hollow out a deep, irregularly shaped piece

PMC can be shaped over ready-made forms in order to give it a domed shape. However, there will be times when you will have a PMC part that will be too deep, or of an irregular or unusual shape that will not work on a preset form. An acorn is a perfect example.

Make a mold of the acorn using your favorite molding material. (Fig. 85)

Fig. 85

Press the PMC into the mold. Any of the types of PMC will work. (Fig. 86)

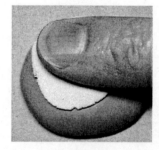

Fig. 86

Remove the PMC from the mold. (Fig. 87)

Fig. 87

Trim the excess PMC from around the acorn. (Fig. 88)

Fig. 88

Set it aside and let it partially dry out. It should be dry enough on the outside so that it can be handled without distorting the shape, yet still be soft on the inside.

Being careful not to break through to the front, hollow the acorn out by digging the PMC from the back. The sides should be about equal to a five card thickness. The PMC that is removed can be wrapped back up with the rest of your stash. (Fig. 89)

Fig. 89

This method can be used to make the finished piece, or it can be used in making parts that will be combined into a single design. If the back will be exposed, then smooth it out by rubbing a little bit of water over it, or by sanding it after it has dried. (Fig. 90) If not, then it is ready to be attached to your design. You can either attach it now, or let it dry completely, then attach it.

Fig. 90

Beads, Hollow Forms, and Cores

There are many items that can be used as cores for beads and hollow forms. The following photographs show some examples of cores, and several samples of beads and the cores that were used.

From left to right: paper clay core covered with several layers of paper towel, wet tissues packed and shaped, cereal, pasta, styrofoam, uncovered paper clay, bread packed and shaped. The plain paper clay core won't shrink so it must be covered with a material that will allow for shrinkage space for the PMC. Wax or wet paper towels or tissues are good for this purpose. All of these core materials are non-toxic when burned, except the styrofoam. The kiln MUST be well ventilated, or set outside, when firing pieces with cores that are toxic when burned. (Fig. 91)

Fig. 91

Paper clay covered with layers of paper towels at least 1/8" thick served as a core for these beads. They are satin finished with a steel wire brush, then oxidized. (Fig. 92)

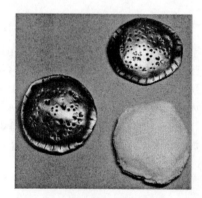

Fig. 92

Fig. 93

Cotton swab ends were the core for these beads. They were heavily oxidized then tumbled to a high polish for an interesting gunmetal blue/black finish. (Fig. 93)

The core for these was Styrofoam. They are satin finished with a steel wire brush, then oxidized. (Fig. 94)

Fig. 94

These beads used wet tissue packed and dried as a core. I tumbled them for a high polish finish. (Fig. 95) Fig. 96 shows a completed necklace.

Fig. 95

Fig. 96

Beads with Paper Clay Cores

Paper clay is wonderful to work with when making cores for beads and hollow pieces. It readily shapes to any form and doesn't sag or misshape as it dries. However, as mentioned earlier, the paper clay core will not shrink, and does not burn away during the firing process. Therefore, it must be covered with another material that is about 1/8" thick to allow room for the PMC to shrink. Covering the paper clay core with wet paper towels or tissues was discussed. For shapes that are irregular and unusual, another more effective technique would be to cover the core with layers of wax.

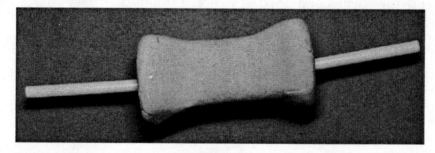

Fig. 97

Fig, 97 shows the plain paper clay core. It was shaped over a stirrer size straw so the holes could be evenly spaced and sized at each end.

This is the paper clay core covered with several layers of wax, built up to about 1/8" thick. It is now ready to be covered with PMC. (Fig. 98)

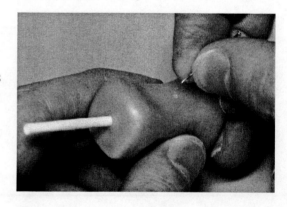

Fig. 98

Bead with Wet Paper Towel Core
Standard PMC, PMC+, or PMC 3

The purpose of this project:

⇒ to make a hollow form
⇒ to learn to use a non-removable core
⇒ to learn to fire a shaped piece

In this project I used a wet paper towel for the core. Paper is not very dense and, therefore, burns off easily with virtually no firing complications. It is also readily available. Tissues can also be used.

Determine the size bead you want. Get a paper towel wet and, squeezing it to pack it down, make the bead to the desired size and shape. You can also wrap the paper towel around an implement, such as a straw or toothpick, in order to make the holes for stringing the bead. I chose to make my holes later. It is purely personal preference. Using a straw or toothpick also makes it easy to hold the bead while you're working on it. When sizing your piece be sure to make the core the 'before firing' size for whichever type of PMC you're using. (Fig. 99)

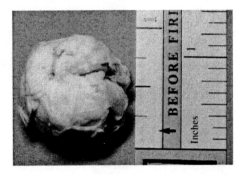

Fig. 99

Roll out a sheet of PMC 4 cards thick. Cut it into triangles (or any shape needed to cover the core form). (Fig. 100) Cover the pieces with a sheet of saran wrap to help keep them from drying out as you're applying each one to the core.

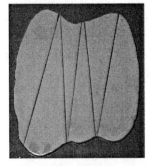

Fig. 100

Cover the core with these pieces. Blend the seams well, making sure to maintain an even thickness of PMC around the entire bead. (Fig. 101)

Fig. 101

Double check to be sure all of the seams have been smoothed. If there are any spots that are obviously thin, add some PMC to these areas and smooth it. (Fig. 102)

Fig. 102

If you haven't already done so, make the holes in the bead. I used a stirrer size drinking straw. (Figs. 103, 104)

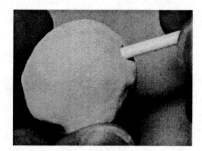

Fig. 103

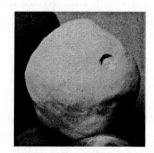

Fig. 104

Depending upon how you will decorate the bead, you can either continue to work on it, or let it dry. If the detail will be intricate it would be a good idea to let the bead dry, in case cracking develops. It is much easier to fill cracks in on an empty bead than to have to redo parts of your design. However, if you can choose to cut or stamp designs, then the PMC must be soft. If there will be carving, then the bead must be completely dry. (I think you get the picture). Now comes the fun! Begin to decorate your bead! Be sure to finish off the holes nicely, too. (Figs. 105, 106, 107, 108)

Fig. 105

Fig. 106

Fig. 107

Fig. 108

After all of the decorating is finished, let the bead completely dry. Sand all rough edges smooth. To prepare the bead for firing, lay it on a small pile of firing support material, either alumina hydrate, or a fine textured vermiculite. (Fig. 109) If you used an implement to support the holes in the beads, it can be removed now. If you choose to leave it in then be SURE it is combustible and will not give off toxic fumes.

Fig. 109

Fire the bead for one of the required firing times and temperatures for the type of PMC you used.

After the bead has been fired you can finish it as desired. I applied a satin finish using the steel wire brush, oxidized it, then high polished some of the details by hand, using a burnisher. (Fig. 110)

Fig. 110

Dragonfly Vase
Standard PMC, PMC+, or PMC3

The purpose of this project:

⇒ to learn to make a vessel
⇒ to work with another type of core material

Any of the three types of PMC will work for this project. The core material used for this vase was floral styrofoam. It is somewhat messy to work with, but is well worth the trouble. It has a fine texture, which lends itself very well to sanding and shaping. The finished measurement of this vase is 2 3/8" tall.

Determine the finished size vase you would like to have. Calculate the enlarged size you will need for the type of PMC you are using. Cut and shape the floral styrofoam to the enlarged, 'before firing' size. (Fig. 111) It may be helpful to extend the top section of the core so you have a handle to hold on to as you're covering it. The core can also be coated with a layer or two of wax, if desired. It may help the PMC to stick better as you're working.

Fig. 111

Working with sheets of PMC rolled 4 cards thick, cover the styrofoam core. Place the vase upside down if the shape of the rim is such that it could sag before drying. Let the vase dry. (Figs. 112, 113)

Fig. 112

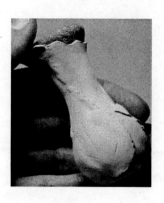

Fig. 113

58

Begin to add the details to your vase. Add the foot. Make sure the foot of the vase is even on the bottom so the vase will stand solidly when finished. When all embellishments have been added, let the vase dry. (Fig. 114)

Fig. 114

After the vase has completely dried, carefully dig the.styrofoam out of the center. (Fig. 115) Sand all rough edges smooth. (Fig. 116)

Fig. 115

Fig. 116

The vase, particularly the rim, needs to be supported during firing so it doesn't sag. Cover the hole in the bottom of a terra cotta flower vase with a small terra cotta chip. Set the vase into the flowerpot. Spoon alumina hydrate around it. (Fig. 117) Notice in the photo that the alumina hydrate does not go all the way up to the rim. As the vase shrinks, it needs a place to go. Since the alimina hydrate does not alter or shift during firing, if it were up to the rim it would be in the way and would distort the original shape of the rim.

Fig. 117

Fire the vase at one of the appropriate firing times and temperatures.

During firing a crack developed in the base of the vase. (Fig. 118) Using PMC+, I filled the crack and re-fired the vase. (Fig. 119) PMC3 can also be used.

Fig.118   **Fig. 119**

To finish the vase I tumbled it, then oxidized it. (Fig. 120)

Fig. 120

Carving and Cutwork
Standard PMC, PMC+, or PMC3

The purpose of this project:

  ⇒ **to transfer a design for carving to the PMC**
  ⇒ **to practice cutwork**
  ⇒ **to practice carving**

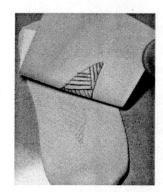

The carved layer will be made first. Using any type of PMC, roll out a sheet 4 to 5 cards thick. The thickness should be determined by how deeply you intend to carve the design. I made a pencil transfer of the design because I have a specific shape in mind for my design. When I transfer this shape in order to accurately cut it out, I transfer the carving design at the same time. (Fig. 121)

Fig. 121

Cut the shape out, then let the PMC completely dry. After the PMC has dried, sand the edges smooth. (Fig. 122) If you haven't already transferred the carving design, then do it now. Since the PMC has dried, the easiest way is to simply draw the design on with a pencil. If the carving lines have been previously transferred but are too light, go over them with a pencil.

Fig. 122

Carve your design. (Fig. 123)m Miniature woodworking carving tools are perfect for this. They come in 1.5mm, 2mm, and 3mm sizes, and five different shapes. A linoleum cutter also works.

Fig. 123

Next, make the cutwork layer. Roll out a sheet of PMC 3 to 4 cards thick. Keep in mind the thickness and weight of the pendant, because the carved layer will be added to the top of this layer.

Lay the carved layer onto the sheet of PMC that you just rolled out. Do the cutwork design, then cut the rest of the shape of the pendant out around the cutwork and carved layer. Lift the carved layer, moisten the PMC slightly, apply PMC slip, replace the carved layer, press firmly, check to be sure it has solidly joined with the bottom layer. (Fig. 124)

Fig. 124

Set the pendant aside to dry.

Add the bail. This bail will be visible from the front of the pendant, but I've chosen to apply it to the back. Roll out a sheet of PMC, 4 cards thick, cut the needed length and width, and lay the bail over a drinking straw. Moisten the back of the pendant with water, smooth the bottom layer of the bail onto the back. (Fig. 125)

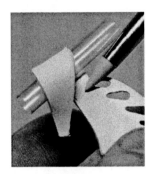

Fig. 125

Add a touch more water, if needed, to the back of the bail. Attach the top layer of the bail. Stamp a design into this layer. Check to be sure there is a strong join. (Fig. 126) Let the bail dry.

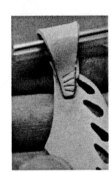

Fig. 126

Finish decorating the front of the bail. Sand any rough edges smooth. (Fig. 127)

Fig. 127

Prepare the pendant for firing. There is some shaping in the bail area on the back of the pendant, so it should be laid on a firing support material. Fire it at one of the times and temperatures specified for the type of PMC you used.

After firing, apply the finish you prefer, then oxidized the piece to enhance the detail of the carving and cutwork. I tumbled the pendant for a high shine, then oxidized it. (Fig. 128) To remove the excess oxidation, rub with a polishing pad. If the oxidation to be removed is heavy, you can use 1200 grit sandpaper, then the polishing pad. Rub with a polishing cloth for the final polishing.

Fig. 128

Simple Bypass Ring
PMC+ or PMC 3

The purpose of this project:

    ⇒ to make a simple ring
    ⇒ to size in ranges

PMC+ and PMC 3 are used for this project because of their strength after firing.

Roll out a sheet of PMC, 5 cards thick. Cut a strip ¼" to 3/8" wide, and 3 3/8" long for a 7, 8, 9 size; 3 1/8" long for a 5, 6, 7 size; and 2 7/8" long for a 3, 4, 5 size. Texture it, or leave it plain. Let it dry. Sand the rough edges. (Fig. 129)

Fig. 129

Fire the ring at 1650F for two hours. This achieves the maximum strength of the PMC.

After firing, carefully shape and size the ring around a ring mandrel. Bend the ring ¼" at a time until you've worked all the way around. Fig. 130) Offset the ends into a bypass design.

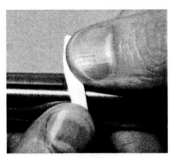

Fig. 130

Tumble to a high shine. This also work hardens the PMC for additional strength. Oxidize, or leave as is. (Fig. 131)

Fig. 131

Ring Set with Cubic Zirconia
Standard PMC, PMC+, or PMC3

The purpose of this project:

⇒ to learn to size a ring
⇒ to set, and fire a cubic zirconia

Any type of PMC can be used for this ring. However, PMC+ and PMC3 will have the most strength.

Cubic zirconia and lab grown corundum stones can be set into the PMC, and fired with the piece because they can withstand the high temperatures of the kiln. Certain other items, such as high-fired ceramic chards, can also be used. It is best to test fire the item if an extra one is available. Otherwise, if there is any doubt, use an alternative method to set it. (Note: Green stones tend to be susceptible to changes during the firing process).

Measure the diameter, in millimeters, of the finger that will wear the ring. Enlarge this measurement according to the type of PMC you are using. A dowel is used for sizing the ring. Use a dowel that is smaller than the enlarged measurement. Cut strips of paper and wrap the layers around the dowel until the correct diameter is achieved. Secure the paper with a piece of scotch tape wrapped completely around it. (Fig. 132) The ring band will be placed on the scotch tape, making it easy to remove from the dowel after it has dried.

Fig. 132

Roll out the PMC, 4 to 5 cards thick. Cut the band the exact width that you need, and the length slightly longer than what is needed. Wrap it around the dowel, being sure it is placed over the scotch tape. Trim the length to fit, and smooth the seam so it is invisible. (Fig. 133)

Fig. 133

Texture the ring band, if desired. (Fig. 134)

Fig. 134

The next step is to set the stones. This ring has a 6mm cubic zirconia in the center, and a 4mm on each side. Cut a brick of PMC the dimensions that you need for your particular stone. This brick measures 7/8" side to side, by 3/8" front to back, by 3/16" deep (a 15 to 16 card thickness). Using a tool that has a diameter slightly smaller then the stones, cut holes all the way through the brick where the stones will be set. (Fig. 135) I used a stirrer size straw. This will let light through from the back of the stone so you get optimum sparkle.

Fig. 135

One at a time, set each stone onto the hole that was cut for it. Press it into the hole. (Fig. 136) When set correctly, the stone should be recessed about 1/16" below the surface of the PMC, and the table (or top, flat part of the stone) should be parallel with the surface. As the PMC shrinks during firing it will grab the widest part of the stone, which will secure it into the setting. It will also push it up slightly, which is why the stone must initially be set slightly below the surface.

Fig. 136

I wanted the stones to be raised above the ring band, so I added 'lifters' to the bottom of the brick. Make an oval from PMC, cut it in half, and apply it to the bottom of the dried PMC brick. (Fig. 137)

Fig. 137

When the lifters have dried, apply the cubic zirconia brick to the ring band. (Fig. 138)

Fig. 138

Add edges, details, and embellishments to the ring. (Fig. 139)

Fig. 139

When the ring is completely dry remove it from the dowel. Fill in any gaps on the inside of the band and sand smooth. (Fig. 140)

Fig. 140

Since this ring band is not completely flat on its sides, it must be laid on a bed of alumina hydrate to preserve the details. (Fig. 141) Fire the ring at one of the appropriate times and temperatures for the type of PMC used.

Fig. 141

After firing I tumbled the ring for a high shine finish. (Figs. 142, 143)

Fig. 142

Fig. 143

Setting Real Stones-Amber
Standard PMC, PMC+, or PMC 3

The purpose of this project:

⇒ to work with bezels
⇒ to set a real stone
⇒ to practice a combination of joining techniques

Any of the three types of PMC can be used for this project. I chose to use standard silver PMC because it is more pliable for the flower designs, and enhances the detail with the amount of shrinkage.

The stone I've chosen to use is amber. Enlarge the stone 132% if using standard PMC, and 112% if using PMC+ or PMC 3. (Fig. 144) This can be done using graph paper, or by enlarging on a copier machine. (Note: There may be slight variances between copier machines. Do a test sample with an inexpensive stone to determine the exact enlargement measurement you should use).

Fig. 144

Trace the outline of the stone on the back of the paper that the enlargement is on. This will have the stone's image facing in the proper direction when it is transferred to the PMC. (Fig. 145)

Fig. 145

Roll out a sheet of PMC 4 cards thick. Place the enlarged photo, pencil tracing down, onto the PMC. Roll over it to transfer the tracing. (Fig. 146)

Fig. 146

Remove the transfer paper from the PMC. (Fig. 147)

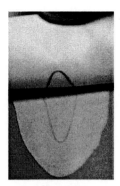

Fig. 147

Cut the desired shape around the transfer. (Fig. 148) This is the base layer for the design.

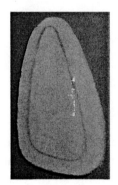

Fig. 148

To make the bezels, roll out a sheet of PMC, 3 cards thick. Using a straight blade, cut a lengthwise edge. This will be the bottom for the bezels. For the amber stone, the bezels need to be ¼" tall. Taper the bezel within this ¼" to a 2 card thickness. Measure the 'before firing' ¼", and cut a straight edge for the top of the bezel. If done correctly, the bezel will be slightly thicker at the bottom than it is at the top. Determine the length bezel that you need for each side of the stone. Cut these lengths. (Fig. 149) Let the PMC dry.

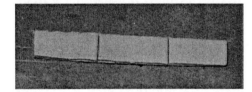

Fig. 149

After the bezel pieces are dry, using a decorative scissors, trim the top edges. (Fig. 150)

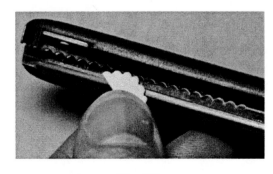

Fig. 150

Apply the bezels to the base layer. Moisten the base layer on the outside edge of the tracing on one of the sides where the bezel will be placed. Join the bezel to the base. Then, on the inside edge of the bezel, apply slip. (Fig. 151) Repeat this method for each of the other sides where there will be bezels. Let them dry.

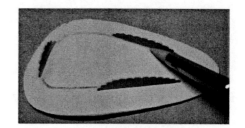

Fig. 151

The bezels at this point can stand on their own, but are not quite strong enough yet. (Fig. 152) They need to be reinforced somehow.

Fig. 152

The bezels can be reinforced by the design that is applied around the perimeter of the stone. Be sure to leave the tops of the bezels accessible so they can be pushed over the stone to hold it in. (Fig. 153)

Fig. 153

When the design is finished, let it dry, then fire it at one of the specified times and temperatures for the type of PMC used.

After firing apply the finish. This piece was tumbled for a high shine, then oxidized. (Fig. 154)

Fig. 154

Solder or epoxy a pin back to the back of the finished piece. Place the stone into the piece. Working around the stone, push the bezels over it until the stone is securely in place. (Fig. 155) I used the end of an old toothbrush as a bezel pusher because, being plastic, it won't mar the amber if I slip while pushing.

Fig. 155

Pendant with Highly Dimensional Glass
Standard PMC, PMC+, or PMC3

The purpose of this project:

⇒ to cut the base and shape the bail, all in one piece
⇒ to drape and fold PMC
⇒ to learn another method to add bezels

This piece of glass proposes a particular challenge because it is highly dimensional, and colorful. (Fig. 156) The setting must be interesting, yet not compete with the character of the glass.

Fig. 156

Enlarge the glass image for the type of PMC you will use. Trace the outline on the back of the enlarged image. Roll out a sheet of PMC, 3 to 4 cards thick, and transfer the image to the PMC. Cut around the pencil transfer, and cut an extension at the top that will be made into the bail. Fold the extension over a drinking straw, drape attractively above the pencil transfer, and, using water, make sure the it is securely joined. Cut the center out to help lighten the weight of the pendant. Fig. 157) Let it dry.

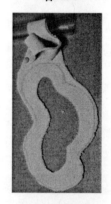

Fig. 157

Add the edges and the bezels. Since the glass piece is so dimensional you must choose the best location for the bezels, and measure the appropriate height. Roll out and cut the bezel pieces. These bezels are attached underneath, then wrapped around the edge to stand straight up, so they are applied when they are cut and the PMC is fresh. (Fig. 158) Let the pendant dry.

Fig. 158

74

Fill the gaps in the back, let it dry, then sand it smooth. (Fig. 159) Fire the pendant at one of the appropriate times and temperatures for the type of PMC used.

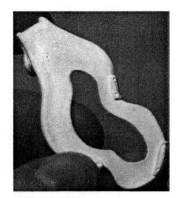

Fig. 159

This pendant was tumbled to a high shine, then oxidized. Set the glass. Using a plastic or wood bezel pusher, push the edges of the bezels over the glass. (Fig. 160) If necessary, add a small amount of epoxy to help secure the glass.

Fig. 160

*glass by pjewelry

75

Link Bracelet with Enamel
PMC+ or PMC 3

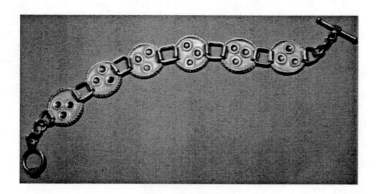

The purpose of this project:

⇒ to make multiple parts
⇒ to join partially dry PMC to dry PMC
⇒ to join dry PMC to dry PMC

Since PMC+ and PMC3 are stronger than standard PMC, the base layers can be made a little thinner. With the addition of the edging, the layered pieces, and finally the enamel, these links will be very strong. Roll out a sheet of PMC+ or PMC3, 3 cards thick. Cut out the number of links for the length bracelet you need. (Fig. 161) Set these aside for the moment.

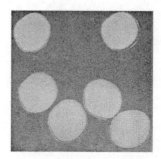

Fig. 161

Roll out another sheet of PMC+ or PMC 3, 3 cards thick. Cut a narrow strip and wrap it lengthwise around a dowel that is 1/16" in diameter. This size tube will nicely accommodate 16 gauge wire, used to join the PMC links together. Smooth the seam and make it slightly flat for easier joining to the bracelet links, then cut sections 1/8" to ¼" long. (Fig. 162) You will need two of these pieces for each link. Let the pieces dry.

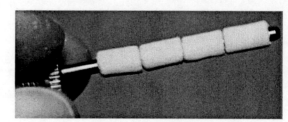

Fig. 162

Make the decorative rings from a sheet rolled two to three cards thick. (Fig. 163) Let them dry to the point where they can be handled without distorting them.

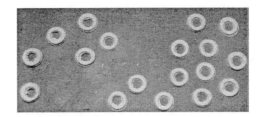

Fig. 163

Apply the rings to the base of each link, using only enough water to make a secure join. (Fig. 164) Let them dry.

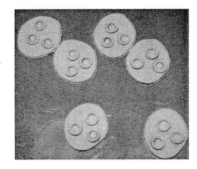

Fig. 164

After both the bracelet links and the tubes are completely dry, join them together.

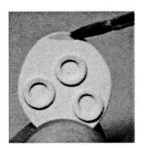

Fig. 165

Fig. 166

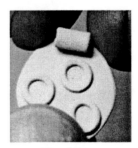

Fig. 167

Moisten the edges of the links and the tubes. (Fig. 165) Apply slip to the tubes. (Fig. 166) Press them together. (Fig. 167) Make sure the joins are solid. Clean any excess slip from around the joins.

Add the edging to each link. (Fig. 168) Texture if desired. Let dry. Sand all rough edges smooth, including the tubes.

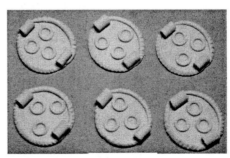

Fig. 168

After the links have dried, fill in any gaps on the back and sand smooth. (Fig. 169)

Fig. 169

Fire the links at 1650F for two hours. This will make both the PMC+ and PMC 3 about as strong as sterling silver. After firing, apply the finish. These links have been tumbled, which work hardens them and adds to their strength. Enamel all of the links. (Fig. 170)

Fig. 170

Join them together with 16 gauge sterling silver wire. Add the clasp. (Fig. 171)

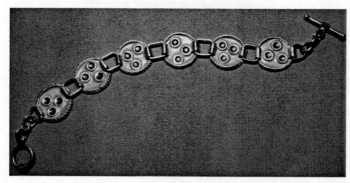

Fig. 171

Cuff Bracelet
PMC+ or PMC3

The purpose of this project:

⇒ to learn layering techniques
⇒ to construct a more advanced design
⇒ to shape a bracelet around a mandrel

PMC+ or PMC3 can be used for this project. The important thing to remember while constructing the bracelet is that it has to be thick enough to be strong, yet not so thick that it is difficult to shape around the bracelet mandrel. This means that the embellishments that are added have to be considered as part of the overall thickness.

Roll out a sheet of PMC+ or PMC3, 4 to 5 cards thick. (Fig. 172) If your will be adding embellishments in the thickness of about 3 cards, then make your bracelet base 4 cards thick. If your embellishments will be thinner, then you can go as thick as 5 cards for the base.

Fig. 172

Cut the length and width needed for your bracelet size. (Fig. 173) This band is cut 1" wide, with the center extending out a little more. The length is 7", which will shrink to approximately 6" to 6 ¼". The PMC+ and PMC3 will shrink roughly 1/8" for each inch.

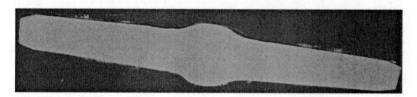

Fig. 173

Add the edges. Roll out a long wire of PMC about 1/8" wide. Moisten the edges of the bracelet base and attach the wires around. Gently press them against the base to make sure they adhere strongly. (Figs. 174, 175)

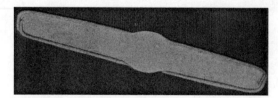

Fig. 174

Fig. 175

Texture the edges, if desired. (Fig. 176) The pressure of the texturing will also help to join the edges solidly to the base.

Fig. 176

After the bracelet has completely dried, fill the gaps in the back. Press full strength PMC (not the slip) into the gaps, then remove as much of the excess as possible. (Fig. 177) Let it dry.

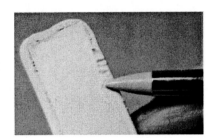

Fig. 177

Using a fine sanding sponge, or sandpaper (grit 1000), sand the back completely smooth. (Fig. 178)

Fig. 178

Embellish the top as desired. (Fig. 179) You will be adding fresh PMC to dry PMC, so use enough water to adhere the parts, being sure to remove the excess. Slip can also be used to adhere the parts, if necessary. Be sure to clean it off completely now, because it will be difficult to sand off later.

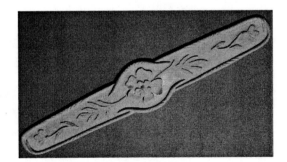

Fig. 179

Let the bracelet dry, then sand any rough edges smooth. Since the bracelet is fired flat and shaped afterwards, lay it on a flat tile, then fire at one of the appropriate times and temperatures for the type of PMC you used.

After the bracelet has been fired, carefully shape it around an oval bracelet mandrel or large dowel. (Fig. 180) Gently but firmly press the bracelet around your form, working around it about ½" at a time.

Fig. 180

Finish the bracelet as desired. I tumbled the bracelet to get a high shine. (Fig. 181) This also work hardens the PMC, which adds to the strength of the piece.

Fig. 181

After the bracelet was tumbled, I oxidized it. (Figs. 182, 183, 184)

Fig. 182

Fig. 183

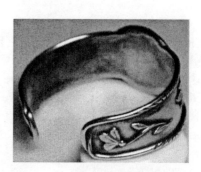

Fig. 184

Firing Silver and 24K Gold PMC Together
Standard Silver and Gold PMC

The purpose of this project:

⇒ to learn to join silver and gold PMC
⇒ to learn about shrinkage of both
⇒ to learn about firing silver and gold together
⇒ to learn about design considerations

When designing a piece that uses both Silver and 24K Gold PMC that will be fired together, the most important thing to remember is that the firing temperatures are different for the two. The standard silver PMC is fired at 1650F, while the 24K gold is fired at 1830F. If the silver PMC is fired at the gold temperature it will melt. Therefore, the only alternative is to fire at the silver firing temperature. This means that, because the gold is fired at the lower temperature of 1650F, which is 90% of its full temperature of 1830F, the gold will reach only about 90% of its full strength. So the strength of the PMC piece will lie in the silver parts. Consequently, the gold PMC should not be placed in the parts of the design that are stress bearing, such as the bail. Or, if it is used on the bail, it should be used decoratively, and placed over silver PMC that will support the gold.

Roll out a sheet of standard silver PMC, 3 to 4 cards thick. Using a pattern that has been made from paper, cut two identical diamond shaped pieces. (Fig. 185)

Fig. 185

Roll out a sheet of gold PMC, 3 cards thick. Cut out two smaller diamond shaped pieces. Moisten the silver PMC and apply the gold PMC on top. (Fig. 186) Make sure the join is solid. Notice in the photo that the paper pattern is still on the gold. That is because it stuck. It doesn't hurt anything to leave the paper on because it will burn away during firing, but I'll have to make another pattern piece. To keep this from happening again, encase the paper pattern between two layers of clear box tape. The pattern can then be easily removed from the PMC, and will be reusable.

Fig. 186

Roll a wire of silver PMC a scant 1/8" in diameter. Position it on one earring, looping it at the top so it can be hung from an earwire. (Fig. 187) Add enough water to secure the two parts together. Repeat the same thing for the second earring. It's best to work one wire at a time. The PMC is at its freshest and is easier to loop. Let the PMC dry, then carve two decorative lines into the gold layer. Sand any rough edges smooth.

Fig. 187

These particular earrings measure just over an expanded 1" on the expanded 'Before Firing' ruler. (Fig. 188)

Fig. 188

Fire the earrings at 1650F for two hours. During firing, the paper that was on the gold has burned away. After firing, they measure just over 1" on the true 6" ruler. (Fig. 189) The silver has its normal white powdery look, and the gold has a yellow powdery look.

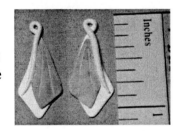

Fig. 189

Even though both the standard silver and the gold PMC have the same shrinkage rate, the silver has actually shrunk the slightest bit more than the gold. This is probably because the gold was fired at 90% of its actual firing temperature, therefore, also shrinking 90%. As a result, a slight doming of the gold has occurred. On these earrings I find it attractive so I left it. The doming can be removed using a rawhide mallet and carefully flattening the piece.

The earrings are satin finished with a steel wire brush, then hand burnished to accent the silver coils, and the carved lines on the gold. Add the earwires. (Fig. 190)

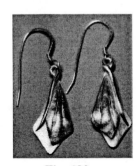

Fig. 190

Adding Fired Gold PMC to PMC+
Standard Gold PMC and PMC+, or PMC3

The purpose of this project:

> ⇒ to work with gold PMC
> ⇒ to attach previously fired PMC to unfired PMC+
> ⇒ to calculate shrinkage using standard PMC and PMC+
> ⇒ to repair cracked PMC+

For this project I chose to use PMC+. However, any of the three types of silver PMC can be used. Just be sure to enlarge each part for the appropriate shrinkage.

Draw a rendering of your design and determine what part will be gold PMC and what will be silver PMC. (Fig. 191) Enlarge the gold parts 30%, and the silver parts 12%.

Fig. 191

Make the gold PMC pieces, being sure to have some way that a mechanical join can form when they are fired into the PMC+. This can be in the form of a small ledge, or holes, or lines. For the little balls I made ledges. The larger sunray piece has angled edges, and the silver PMC+ will also overlap the top point. Sand smooth the edges that will be exposed. Fire the gold at 1830F for two hours. (Fig. 192) Or, since the gold is not in a stress bearing part of the design it could be fired at a lower temperature. When I fired some of my standard silver PMC pieces at 1650F I also fired the gold. The gold will be 90% of its strength at this temperature. Since the gold is not in a stress bearing part of the design, such as the bail, this method works. I wouldn't recommend firing the gold any lower.

Fig. 192

Roll a sheet of PMC+ 3 cards thick. Cut the first diamond shaped layer, and place the previously fired gold sunray onto the PMC+. (Fig. 193) Press the top part of the gold into the PMC+. Leave the bottom part of the rays sitting on top. This will allow the PMC+ to shrink beneath the gold PMC. If the bottom of the rays are embedded the gold will buckle as the PMC+ shrinks. (You'll see evidence of this later in the project). Let this layer dry.

Fig. 193

Roll a sheet of PMC+ 3 cards thick. Cut out the second diamond shaped layer. Moisten this layer with a small amount of water, add some PMC+ slip, and attach the first layer on top of this layer. (Fig. 194) Let the second layer dry. Sand the rough edges smooth.

Fig. 194

From a PMC+ sheet 3 cards thick, cut a strip for a bail about 3/16" to ¼" wide and long enough to wrap around a drinking size straw. This will be a base for the decorative coils. Attach the bail to the pendant. Add an extra PMC+ ray to the left edge of the sunray. (Fig. 195) Let these parts dry.

Fig. 195

Add the coils to the support bail. Using a needle tool make holes where the three gold balls will go. Press the balls into the holes making sure the ledges are deep enough that they will be concealed when the PMC+ shrinks. (Fig. 196)

Fig. 196

Cracks can develop in the coils as they are being shaped. Don't panic. After the coils dry use PMC+ clay (not slip) to fill in the cracks. Let it dry. (Figs. 197, 198)

Fig. 197   Fig. 198

Using a fine sanding sponge, or 1000 grit sandpaper, sand the area smooth. (Figs. 199, 200)

Fig. 199   Fig. 200

This piece measures about 2 1/8" before firing. (Fig. 201) Fire the pendant at one of the recommended times and temperatures for PMC+. After firing the piece measures about 1 7/8". (Fig. 202)

Fig. 201   Fig. 202

Because I had the entire gold piece embedded, it caused buckling as the silver PMC shrank. (Fig. 203) So I wouldn't mar the metal, I used a rawhide hammer and a toothbrush handle to carefully flatten the bulge. Sometimes it flattens nicely, sometimes it doesn't. In this case most of it flattened well, except for a small area

towards the top of the gold piece. An unattractive angle formed, so I made a little, silver PMC flower with a gold center and attached it to the pendant. (Fig. 204) The flower can be soldered, or attached with a strong epoxy.

Fig. 203

Fig. 204

PMC Sheet

Pin with Dichroic Glass

The purpose of this project:

⇒ **to experience PMC sheet**

PMC sheet is very, very thin. It is about equal to rolling out PMC, 1 card thick. What is unique about this sheet is that it is specially formulated not to dry out fast. This makes it easy to mold, and can be worked for an extended period of time. The folds that I made for this pin were soft and pliable even after two days!

For this project, PMC+ or PMC3 can be used in conjunction with the PMC sheet. They all have the same shrinkage rate and firing specifications.

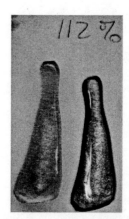

Enlarge the image of the glass piece 112%. (Fig. 205) On the back of the paper, pencil trace the outline of the enlarged glass image.

Fig. 205

Roll out a sheet of PMC+ or PMC3, 3 to 4 cards thick, then transfer the pencil tracing to the PMC. (Fig. 206) This is the base for the pin. Cover the base with plastic wrap so it doesn't dry out.

Fig. 206

Using the PMC sheet, form the folds of the drape. Moisten the base sheet next to the pencil transfer. then apply the folded PMC sheet onto it. (Fig. 207) Be sure there is a good join. Cut out around the pencil tracing and remove the excess PMC. (Another method would be to fold the PMC sheet first, roll out the PMC+ or PMC3 base, and then apply the folded sheet to the base sheet).

Fig. 207

Make the bezels, apply them, secure them, then add the rest of the details. (Fig. 208) Let the piece dry. The PMC+ and PMC3 will dry faster than the PMC sheet. Sand all rough edges, being careful not to damage the PMC sheet if it is still soft. Fire the piece at one of the appropriate times and temperatures for the PMC used.

Fig. 208

Finish the piece as desired. This pin is satin finished with a steel wire brush. The details are burnished by hand. (Fig. 209)

Fig. 209

Set the glass. (Fig. 210) Use a plastic or wood bezel pusher to push the edges of the bezels over the glass.

Fig. 210

*glass by pjewelry

An Interesting Section For Potters

PMC Applied to Glazed Ceramic Tiles
Low fire glazes

In these experiments I used standard PMC and PMC+ on tiles that had low-fired glazes on them. The glazes were fired onto the tiles at approximately 2000 degrees Fahrenheit. For the first two experiments the tiles were laid flat during firing. For the third experiment, the tile was placed vertically, simulating what would happen if PMC were applied to the side of a vessel.

Experiment 1 –Using standard PMC

First, I took a fresh piece of PMC, pressed it into a small mold, released it from the mold, and immediately applied it to a broken piece of tile that had a low fire glaze on it. I applied the molded PMC by smoothing the excess PMC around the edges onto the glazed tile. This way I tested what would happen if an appliqué was attached to a glazed pot, and also how a thin layer of slip would work.

I then took the same mold, pressed fresh PMC into it, released it from the mold, trimmed off all of the excess PMC around the shape, let it dry, and then attached it to the glazed tile using PMC slip.

Fig. 211

The tile was fired flat at 1650F for 2 hours. The results: in both instances, there was very strong adhesion of the PMC to the glazed tile. (Fig. 211)

Further observations – A clear layer of glaze "seeped" over, and covered, the thin edges that had been smoothed onto the tile around the PMC mold. Therefore, the white look as it comes from the kiln would have to remain because the PMC could not be shined or finished in any way. The trimmed mold that was dried, then applied with slip, had very clean edges.

Experiment 2 –Using PMC+

Fig. 212

Using the same mold as for the first experiment, I pressed PMC+ into it, released it from the mold, cut the excess PMC+ off, let it dry, then attached it to the low fire glazed tile with PMC+ slip.

Separately, I applied PMC+ slip in varying thickness, thin to heavy, directly onto the glazed tile. The tile was then fired flat at the lower temperature of 1470F for 30 minutes.

The results: there was very strong adhesion in both instances. The dried, molded piece of PMC+ that was applied had very clean edges. The glaze from the tile did not "seep" onto the slip. Even the thin areas of slip were exposed and able to be finished. (Fig. 212)

Experiment 3 –Using PMC+

In the third experiment I used PMC+, and applied the mold and the slip in the same way as in experiment two. This time the tile was fired vertically at 1650F for two hours. The results: the adhesion of both applications was very strong. The molded PMC+ that was applied did not sag (it extended from the surface about 3/16"). Once again, the glaze "seeped" onto the thinner areas of slip, therefore rendering them unable to be finished. It actually created a very interesting look, between the thinner areas of slip that couldn't be finished, and the thicker areas that could. (Fig. 213)

Fig. 213

PMC Applied to Glazed Ceramic Tiles
High Fire Glazes

In each of these experiments standard PMC and PMC+ were applied to sample tiles that had high fire glazes applied to them, and had been fired at approximately 2200F-- 2400F. All of the tiles were fired vertically, which would simulate applying PMC to the side of a mug, vase, or other types of vessels.

Experiment 1—Using Standard PMC

I first pressed PMC into a mold, let it dry, then, using PMC slip, applied it to the sample tile with the high fire glaze on it. I then applied slip, in varying thickness, to the tile and let it dry. I placed the tile into the kiln vertically and fired it at 1650F for 2 hours. I let the kiln cool naturally before removing the tile.

With a little pressure from my fingers, the mold I had applied popped off. I reapplied the now fired PMC mold to the surface of the tile using more slip, and also made the slip thicker (a little stiffer than a toothpaste consistency would be). I re-fired the tile at 1650F for 2 hours. This time after firing the PMC applied mold had very strong adhesion. (Fig. 214)

Fig. 214

The PMC slip had very strong adhesion in most areas. The areas of the slip that had not been as carefully or "securely" applied were more apt to peel away from the surface of the glazed tile.

The glaze did not seep over the PMC, so the silver could be finished and shined if desired.

Experiment 2—Using PMC+

I pressed two molds using PMC+, immediately applying one to the sample tile with PMC+ slip and feathering the edges (the same as slip would be applied). The second mold I let dry, then applied it to the tile using ample slip, but not so much that it oozed out from the edges. I fired the tile vertically at 1650F for 10 minutes, then let the kiln cool naturally.

There was very strong adhesion in both mold applications. The glaze did not seep over the PMC+, so the silver could be finished and shined if desired. (Fig. 215)

Fig. 215

Experiment 3—Using PMC+

Fig. 216

I again pressed PMC+ from a mold, let it dry, then applied it to the sample tile using PMC+ slip. I also applied PMC+ slip in varying thickness. The tile was fired at 1470F for 30 minutes, and the kiln let to cool naturally.

There was very strong adhesion in both applications. The PMC+ was not covered by glaze so could be finished and shined, if desired. (Fig. 216)

PMC3 Applied to Glazed Tiles

I first adhered fresh PMC3 to a low fire glazed tile and a high fire glazed tile, then fired them at 1110F for 30 minutes. After this first firing the PMC3 did not adhere to the high fire glaze tile. Now already fired, I tried re-applying the PMC3 piece to the high glazed tile at both 1200F and 1290F. The results are as follows.

Low fire glaze tile with PMC3 (Fig. 217) fired at:

1110F for 30 minutes: PMC3 adhered fairly well. Some of the edges where it had been applied thinner, wanted to peel off. These were areas where the PMC3 had not been as securely applied as in other areas.

1200F for 20 minutes: I added just a little more PMC3 slip to the areas that wanted to peel off. At this temperature the adhesion was strong, even around the edges.

1290F for 10 minutes: Strong adhesion.

Fig. 217

High fire glaze tile with PMC3 (Fig. 218) fired at:

1110F for 30 minutes: PMC3 did not adhere at all.

1200F for 20 minutes: Re-adhered the fired PMC3 piece with fresh PMC3. Re-fired. PMC3 did not adhere at all.

1290F for 10 minutes: Re-adhered the fired PMC3 piece with fresh PMC3. Re-fired. PMC3 still did not adhere.

Fig. 218

Raku glaze

A student of mine had some small ceramic pieces to which she had applied a Raku glaze. To one piece she applied a fresh PMC design, using PMC slip. To the second piece she added a fired piece of PMC, using PMC slip. We fired the pieces at 1650F for two hours. After firing we quenched the pieces. The PMC parts that had been applied fell off of both glazed pieces. Using PMC slip, she re-applied the same PMC pieces to the Raku glazed pieces. (Now both applied PMC pieces had been fired). This time, after firing at 1650F for two hours, I opened the kiln door halfway and let the pieces cool gradually. The adhesion of the PMC to the Raku glazed pieces was clean and very strong.

Final Observations

From all of these experiments I have concluded that it is actually the glaze that holds the PMC on. The minimum requirement for the low fire glaze is the PMC3 firing temperature and time of 1200F for 20 minutes. The minimum requirement for the high fire glaze is 1470F for 30 minutes. There was no reaction with the silver that might cause discoloration or other changes. The glaze itself remained unaltered.

The raku glaze was tested the same as the low fire glazes, with the same results. An interesting observation was noted: the raku was 'cleaned up' after the PMC firing. In other words, the effect of the carbon on the glaze in its original firing disappeared when it was re-fired.

Other Interesting Notes

I applied PMC, in the same manner as the previous experiments, to a box made of unglazed terracotta clay. It did not adhere well at all.

I also mixed PMC with white porcelain clay to see if the PMC would strengthen it. It took a mixture of at least 75% PMC and 25% porcelain clay before any noticeable difference was made. And the color became a very unattractive, muddy brown.

I have performed these experiments in the hopes that some adventurous potters would be curious enough to add another dimension to their work. Are you ready?

Resources

United States

Rio Grande
7500 Bluewater Road NW
Albuquerque, NM 87121-1962
800-545-6566
www.riogrande.com

PMC Connection
3718 Cavalier Drive
Garland, TX 75042
800-PMC-Clay
www.pmcconnection.com

Silver Clay
3300 Girant NE
Albuqueruqe, NM 67107
800-781-2529
www.silver-clay.com

Cano and Fenley
P.O. Box 14928
Albuquerque, NM 87191-4928
www.MetalClay.com

PMC Guild
417 W. Mountain Avenue
Fort Collins, CO 80521
www.pmcguild.com

Pjewelry
www.pjewelry.com

United Kingdom and Eire

www.silveralchemy.co.uk

Germany

www.c-hafner.de
Japan

Mitsubishi Materials Corporation of Japan –
manufacturer of PMC
www.mmc.co.jp

Korea

Myong Hwa & Co., Ltd.
629-31 Shinsa-Dong
Kangnam-ku, Seoul 135-120
Korea

Index

Alumina hydrate, 17, 26, 31, 57, 59
Applying findings, 36

Beads, 52, 53, 54, 55
Bezels, 71, 72, 74, 91
Bracelets, 76, 80

Care of, 27
Carving, 18, 62
Core materials, 25, 52, 53, 54, 58
Characteristics, 11
Cutwork, 18, 62

Designing, 37
Draping, 15, 24, 74, 90

Equipment, 30

Firing, 30
    Supplies, 17
    Preparing pieces for firing, 31
    Firing chart, 32
    Two-tone pieces, 33, 84, 86
Finishes
    High shine, 16, 34
    Satin, 16, 35
    Oxidizing/patina, 35
    Enameling, 35, 78
Forming Techniques, 22
    Joining, 23, 24, 41, 77
    Texturing, 15, 43, 45
    Embellishing, 24, 46, 47
    Folding, 24
Forms of PMC, 10, 20
    Lump clay, 10
    Syringe, 10, 24
    Sheet, 10, 90
    Paste, 10

Glazes
    Ceramic High Fire, 96, 98
    Ceramic Low Fire, 94, 98
    Raku, 98

Hollow Forms, 25, 55, 58

Kiln, 30
    Set-up, 30
    Loading, 32
    Operating, 32

Properties of, 10
PMC ruler, 10
Projects, 39

Repairing, 27, 60, 88
Refining, 26, 88
Re- hydrating, 21
Rings, 65, 66

Setting stones, 66, 70
Soldering, 27
Sanding, 15, 26, 27
Shrinkage, 10, 12, 85, 86, 87
Slip, 14, 22, 24

Types of PMC
    Standard, 10, 11
      Silver, 10
      Gold, 10
    PMC+, 10, 11
    PMC3, 10, 11
Tools, 14

Vermiculite, 17, 26, 31

ISBN 155369470-8